WHAT ON EARTH?

BEES

Andrea Quigley
Pau Morgan

Contents

Dance like a bee on page 23.

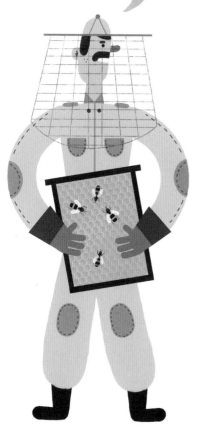

Find out what beekeepers do with honey on page 32.

Make a nectar café on page 18.

Make your own
fuzzy bee
on page 42.

Grow wild flowers
to attract bees
on page 52.

Saving bees

Make a water dish
for thirsty bees
on page 55.

Bee stings and allergies

- If stung by a bee, remove the sting and seek medical attention.
- If the person stung feels sick, dizzy or faint, or is allergic to bee venom, seek urgent medical attention.
- Anyone with a known serious allergy to bee venom should seek medical advice before going near bees and ensure they have access to epinephrine (adrenaline).

Bee poems

Imagine how it feels to be a bee.

How doth the little busy bee

How doth the little busy bee
improve each shining hour,
and gather honey all the day
from every open flower!

How skilfully she builds her cell!
How neat she spreads the wax!
And labours hard to store it well
with the sweet food she makes.

ISAAC WATTS (1674–1748)

Busy bee

Happily I buzz loudly in the sun
Visiting flowers one by one
Seeking sweet nectar - yum, yum, yum!
I will fly all day until my work is done.

Can you write a bee poem?

Say hello to bees

Around two hundred million years ago, there were no flowers and no bees. Big tough plant-eating dinosaurs roamed the earth, eating big tough plants.

Slowly things began to change. It took millions of years for the plants to start producing small, pale flowers.

Beetles and flies began to visit the flowers to eat their yummy **pollen** grains.

Around 130 million years ago wasps appeared. The wasps ate the insects on the flowers, but they also liked pollen. Some wasps liked it so much that they stopped eating insects and turned into bees.

Bees grew hair on their bodies to help carry pollen from plant to plant.

Bees helped more flowers to grow by carrying pollen from one flower to another (see pages 14–15). Flowers started developing scents and large, coloured petals to attract the bees. They produced sweet, runny **nectar** for bees to feed on.

Did you know?

The oldest bee fossil ever found is from 100 million years ago. It still looks a bit like a wasp but younger fossils (from about 50 million years ago) show bees just like the ones we have today.

All types of bees

Now there are lots of different bees around the world including **honey bees, solitary bees, bumble bees,** and **stingless bees.**

Red dwarf honey bee

Western honey bee

Giant honey bee

Tawny mining bee

Honey bees

Honey bees live in large **colonies** making **honey**. Most honey bees are looked after by beekeepers, but there are some that live in the wild. Male **drones** and female **worker bees** work for the **queen bee**. There are only seven species.

Leafcutter bee

Hairy footed flower bee

Solitary bees

Solitary bees live alone or in small groups of individual nests. They each have special wild flowers that they like to visit. Solitary bees eat only pollen and nectar. There are about 19,200 species.

When you see a bee, take a long look. Draw a picture and see if you can find out what type of bee it is.

But remember! Don't get too close to us bees. We like to be left alone – and some of us do sting!

Common carder bee

Red tailed bumble bee

American bumble bee

Bumble bees

Bumble bees are fat, round and furry. They live in the wild in small colonies with a queen. They make tiny pots of watery honey in their nests, just enough to feed the queen and her **larvae** but not enough for humans to eat! There are around 250 species.

Sugar bag bee

Xunan kab or Royal lady bee

Jataí bee

Stingless bees

Stingless bees live in tropical regions of Asia, Australasia and South America. They make honey and live in colonies. They bite to protect themselves but they can't sting. There are about 500 to 600 species (see page 49).

Parts of a bee

Bees are insects, so they don't have bones like we do. They have a tough shell on the outside of their body, called an exoskeleton. Like all insects, bees have six legs and their body is divided into three parts: the head, thorax and abdomen. This is a honey bee, but all bees have the same parts.

Proboscis

The bee's long tongue is called a **proboscis**. It can suck nectar and water.

Ocelli

These three small eyes, called ocelli, help the bee fly the right way up.

Compound eyes

The huge eyes on either side of the head are called compound eyes. They are made up of thousands of smaller eyes (see pages 20-21).

Antennae

A bee uses its antennae to feel, taste and smell its way around the dark hive, to explore flowers and to greet other bees.

Mandibles

A bee uses its jaws, called **mandibles**, to chew pollen and to shape the **wax** it uses to build its hive. Some solitary bees chew leaves or wood to make their nests instead.

Wings

A bee's fore wing and hind wing are hooked together to make a large, powerful wing so bees can fly fast and accurately. Wings are also used to fan and cool the hive.

Pollen baskets

Honey bees and bumble bees use 'pollen baskets' on their legs to carry the pollen back to their hive. These stiff hairs are especially good for collecting pollen. Solitary bees carry pollen on long hairs under their abdomen instead.

Feet

A bee also uses its feet to feel, taste and smell its world. A bee's feet can feel when another bee is doing the waggle dance (see page 22).

Spiracles

Bees don't have lungs in their chests like we do. Instead they have ten holes, called spiracles, along each side of their body. They can breathe through these, filling air sacs inside the body.

Sting

Only female bees have a sting. It defends her from creatures that are after her honey or threaten her colony.

The game of life

There are four main stages of a bee's life cycle: **egg**, larva, **pupa** and adult bee. See how long it takes you to grow into an adult honey bee in this game!

Toolkit
- Dice
- Paper counters and coloured pens/pencils
- Some friends!

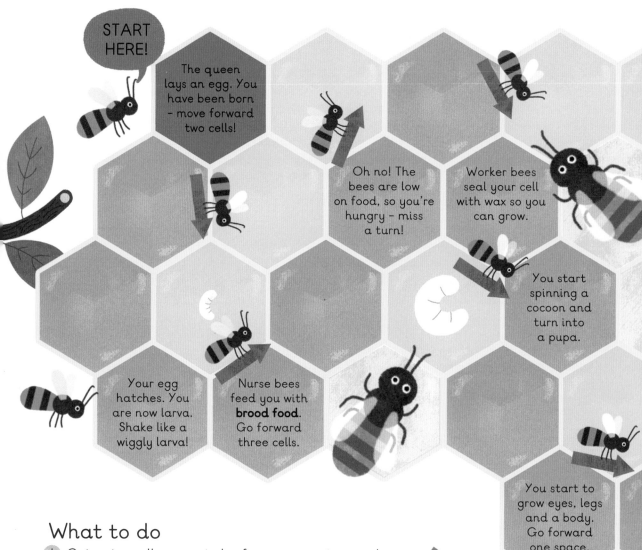

START HERE!

The queen lays an egg. You have been born – move forward two cells!

Oh no! The bees are low on food, so you're hungry – miss a turn!

Worker bees seal your cell with wax so you can grow.

You start spinning a cocoon and turn into a pupa.

Your egg hatches. You are now larva. Shake like a wiggly larva!

Nurse bees feed you with **brood food**. Go forward three cells.

You start to grow eyes, legs and a body. Go forward one space.

What to do
1. Cut out small paper circles for your counters and paint them different colours for each player.
2. Take it in turns to roll the dice and move forward by the number rolled. Stick to the yellow path and follow the instructions on each cell.
3. The first player to turn into a bee wins!

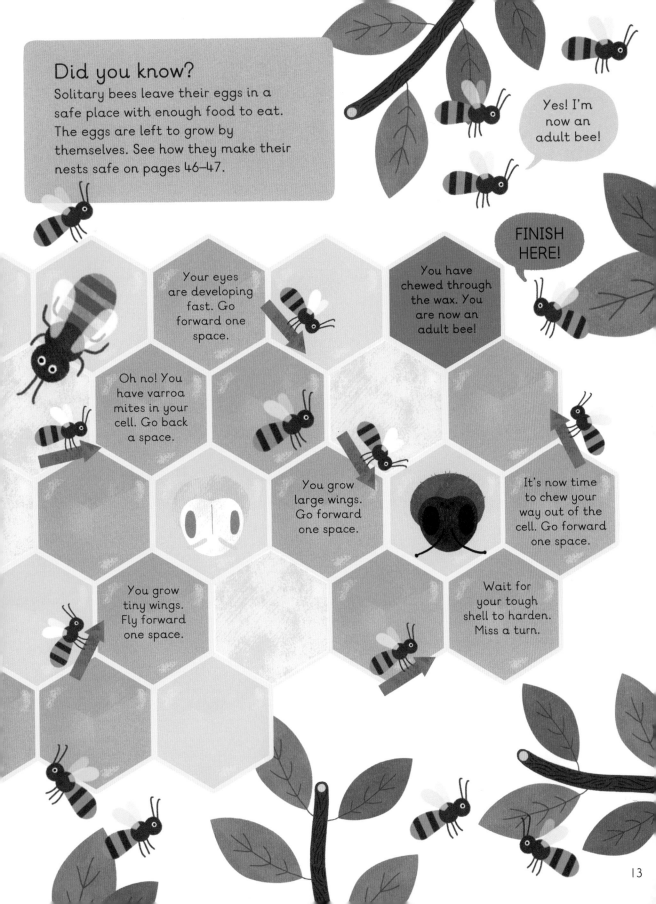

Did you know?

Solitary bees leave their eggs in a safe place with enough food to eat. The eggs are left to grow by themselves. See how they make their nests safe on pages 46–47.

Yes! I'm now an adult bee!

FINISH HERE!

Your eyes are developing fast. Go forward one space.

You have chewed through the wax. You are now an adult bee!

Oh no! You have varroa mites in your cell. Go back a space.

You grow large wings. Go forward one space.

It's now time to chew your way out of the cell. Go forward one space.

You grow tiny wings. Fly forward one space.

Wait for your tough shell to harden. Miss a turn.

Food to eat

When you think of bees, you might think of yummy honey but bees help provide a lot of the food we eat, including most fruit and nuts. Bees are part of the magical process called **pollination.**

nectaries

anther

stigma

Pollen is made by the part of the flower called the **anther. Nectaries** at the base of the flower produce nectar.

The bee flies to another flower to drink more nectar. Pollen from her body brushes onto the flower's **stigma.**

Pollen and nectar are foods for bees. Pollen provides protein to help bees grow and nectar is rich in sugars for energy.

Bees gather the pollen in their pollen baskets or in the long hairs under their abdomen. They drink the nectar with their tongues (see pages 24–25).

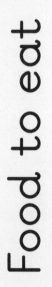

The pollen from the bee goes down the stigma to the centre of the flower. The flower is **fertilized** and makes **seeds**. A fruit or nut grows around the seeds, then the flower dies. Animals eat the tasty fruit and nuts, helping to spread the seeds around so that new plants can grow.

fruit

Did you know?
Bees, butterflies, hover flies and beetles, birds, bats and the wind, can all move pollen between flowering plants.

Nectar smells delicious!

seeds

We need bees to pollinate flowers so that we have lots of fruit and nuts to eat.

15

Bee a pollinator

Bees fly between flowers to gather pollen and nectar as food to eat. As they feed, they pollinate the flowers. Which flowers are the best to feed from and to pollinate?

Toolkit

- Paper
- Sticky tape
- Coloured pencils, pens or crayons and a notepad
- Paintbrush
- Glitter
- Different types of flowers

What to do

1 Ask your adult to help you trace and cut out a bee from the template on page 60. Use sticky tape to stick your bee to the top of your paintbrush.

2 Look at your flower's shape. Is it open and saucer-like or closed up with lots of petals?

3 Dip your paintbrush in the glitter and try to paint the glitter into the centre of the flower. Repeat this on a different flower.

Try flowers with different shapes!

4 Draw the shape of each flower in your notebook and record how much glitter is in the centre of the flower. Which flower was the easiest to reach or the most difficult?

What happens?
Watch how much glitter reaches the middle of the flowers. Bees find it easier to reach the heart of open single flowers like daisies, so they are easily pollinated. Bees find it difficult to find pollen and nectar in 'fancy' flowers with many rows of petals. Fancy flowers aren't often found in the wild.

In China, farmers use huge paint brushes to pollinate flowers...

...because their bees have disappeared.

Chinese bees
Bees in Southwest China died out because they had nowhere to nest, too few plants for food and too much **insecticide**. Today, Chinese farmers have to do the bees' work themselves! They dab pollen on to fruit trees with brushes.

Make a nectar café

Bees are always searching for flowers to feed from. What colour flower do they like the best? Make your own nectar café to find out!

This outdoor experiment is best done on a warm and sunny summer's day.

Toolkit

- Thick card
- Paint, pencils or crayons
- Cling film® or sticky plastic wrap
- Sponge
- Glue
- Sugar and water
- Drawing pin
- Cane or stick
- Tracing paper
- Sticky tape
- Ruler
- Scissors

What to do

1. Trace the flower template on page 60 and transfer it onto thick card. Cut out your flower shape. Make five flowers.

2. Paint your flowers. Make one flower red, one yellow, one blue and then two more with any colours you like. You can also try using patterns of colour.

3. Cover the flower with cling film and secure with sticky tape (or laminate it).

Nectar is my favourite food!

4 Ask your adult to help you fix a drawing pin through the centre of the flower onto the end of a cane or stick. This stick will be your flower stalk. Use some sticky tape if needed to help hold the pin in place.

5 Cut out a circle about 2cm across from a piece of sponge. Glue the sponge to the centre of the flower and leave the glue to set hard overnight.

6 Mix a teaspoon of sugar in a cup of water. Then drip some of this sugar water onto the sponge in the centre of the flower.

7 Stick the flowers outside. Watch to see how many bees visit each flower.

What happens?
Bees like lots of different flowers but many prefer yellow, blue or violet flowers. These are the colours that bees can see the best (see pages 20-21). Flowers that use bees to pollinate are often yellow, blue or violet to attract them.

Don't forget to provide water at your café - see page 55.

Did you know?
Lots of other insects love nectar. It's an important food source with lots of **carbohydrates**. You might see butterflies, moths, hover flies and even beetles visit your nectar café!

Bee vision

Bees have remarkable eyesight. They have two different types of eyes – each has a job to do.

Compound eyes

These two large eyes are actually made up of many little eyes that work together. They help bees fly fast and in the right direction without crashing into anything.

Ocelli

The three smaller eyes in the centre of a bee's head help bees see light and stay the right way up.

Bee purple

Like people, bees see in colour. We see red, yellow and blue and all the colours in between, just like a rainbow. Bees are good at seeing yellow, blue and violet but can't see red. Red objects look black or grey to them. But bees are special and can see **ultra-violet (UV) light.** Humans can't see UV light – we call it 'bee purple'.

I can see red!

flower in daylight

I can see bee purple!

flowers in UV light

Mosaic flowers

Each small eye in the compound eye views one part of a giant picture – a bit like a mosaic. See like a bee and design a mosaic flower for bees to land on.

Toolkit

- White card
- Purple paper scraps of different shades
- Yellow paper scraps
- Ruler
- Pencil
- Scissors
- Glue stick

What to do

1 With your adult, cut the paper scraps into square, rectangle and triangle 'tiles'.

2 Draw a flower on to the white card. (You can use the template on p60.)

3 Using your glue stick, fix each paper tile on to your flower. Now you can see like a bee!

Bee purple helps bees find nectar in the flower.

Did you know?

Some flowers have special 'bee purple' markings called 'bee lines' to show bees the best place to land to reach the pollen and nectar. What helpful flowers!

21

Finding sweet nectar

When a honey bee finds some nectar, she brings it back to the hive and lets her sister bees taste it. If it is good nectar, then they will want to collect some more!

How do they know where to go?

Bees communicate by dancing! If a bee thinks the nectar is good she will dance excitedly. The other bees will notice and join in her dance.

If the food is nearby, she will dance in a circle – called the round dance.

We're dancing in a circle.

Bees use the waggle dance to find food that is far away.

If the food is far away, she will dance in a figure of eight – called the waggle dance. The middle line in the figure of eight shows the bees the direction of where to go. The length of time the bee shakes her abdomen tells them how far to fly.

Here they are!

Do the bee dance

Can you help your friends find some tasty treats?

What to do

First, choose an area to be the hive. This is where you will dance and play music. Hide your treats in two places – some nearby and others further away.

Toolkit
- Music
- Tasty treats
- Some friends!

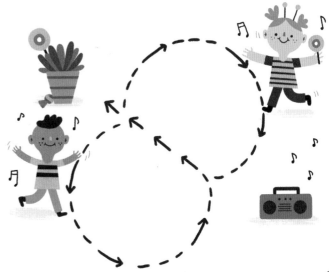

The round dance

In your hive, give your friends one of the tasty treats you have hidden nearby. Dance around in a circle. Waggle your bottom every few paces, just like a bee. Your friends need to follow you in your dance. When the music stops, you all 'fly' from the hive until you find the tasty treats.

The waggle dance

In your hive, give your friends one of the tasty treats you have hidden further away. Dance around in a figure of eight. The middle line of your 'eight' should point to where the treat is hidden. Your friends need to follow you in your dance. When the music stops, you all 'fly' from the hive, in the direction of the midline, until you find the tasty treats.

23

Drink like a bee

Bees use their tongues (called a proboscis) to suck sweet nectar from flowers into their stomachs. The tongue looks like a drinking straw. See if you can drink like a bee!

Toolkit

- Drinking straws
- Scissors
- Saucer
- Cup
- Tall beaker
- Teaspoon
- Water

What to do

1 Ask your adult to help you cut the drinking straws into three different lengths: 3cm, 6cm (or the length of the cup) and one full length.

2 Pour a teaspoon of water into each container.

3 Choosing one straw at a time, put it in your mouth and use your lips to hold it tight. Try to drink the water from each container, without using your hands!

Which straw works best with which container?

What happens?

- The short straw is easy to use with the saucer but too small for the tall beaker or cup.
- The medium straw is easy to use with the cup but too small for the tall beaker.
- The long straw can reach to the bottom of the beaker but is hard to control with the saucer and cup.

Tawny mining bee

Hairy footed flower bee

Bumble bee

Find the best flower

Flowers are different shapes and sizes – like your containers. Different types of bees have tongues of different lengths – like your straws. Follow the path of each bee to see which type of flower they like.

Bees around the world

There are lots of different types of bees that live around the world. Here are just some of them:

American sweat bees have shiny metallic coloured bodies that shimmer in the light.

NORTH AMERICA

Squash bees pollinate pumpkin and squash flowers in the morning. At night the male squash bees sleep inside the flowers.

CENTRAL AMERICA

The Ancient Mayans worshipped the bee god *Ah-Muzen-Cab*. They kept stingless bees and used the honey as medicine. They called their bees the Royal lady or *Xunan kab*. Today, Central Americans still value their honey highly.

SOUTH AMERICA

Stingless bees have a queen, worker bees and drones, just like honey bees. However, Jetaí bees in South America have four types of bee, including the guard bee.

Western honey bees were brought by European people to America in the 1620s, to Australia in the 1820s, and to New Zealand in the 1850s.

The bumble bee *Bombus impetuosus* lives in the Sichuan mountains of China. These furry bees can fly even higher than the world's tallest mountain.

The giant honey bee (17-20mm long) lives in the high mountains of Nepal. Men climb huge rock faces to collect the honey. It is very dangerous work.

EUROPE

ASIA

The world's biggest bee is Wallace's giant bee. From head to tail the female is 39mm long but her wings measure 63mm from tip to tip.

AFRICA

Bees came from Africa about 100 million years ago. Today, 25,000 kinds of bee live throughout the world, except for Antarctica.

The world's smallest bee *Quasihesma clypearis* is only 1.8mm long. She is so small you would only notice her if you saw her shadow moving.

INDONESIA

AUSTRALIA

Bees make honey from the Manuka plant, which is used to heal wounds and treat illnesses in hospitals today.

NEW ZEALAND

Honey bees

There can be thousands of honey bees in any one colony. There is only one queen and lots of workers. Each bee has a special role to play:

The queen bee

There is only one queen bee. She is the largest bee and mother to all the bees in her colony. She lays up to 2,000 eggs a day. She can live for one to three years. Queens used to live for as long as six years but it is now rare for them to survive this long.

The drone

Male bees are called drones. The drone's only job is to mate with the queen bee. A drone has huge eyes to help find the queen and large, powerful wings to fly fast to catch her. Every winter, the worker bees throw out any drones who are eating precious honey instead of mating with the queen. In the cold and without food the drones soon die.

The worker bee

Female worker bees do all the work in the hive. They look after the queen and the young bees. They make honey, guard the hive and fetch food. Workers bees do each job in turn until they become foragers who fetch food. They work so hard in the summer that they only live for six weeks but in the winter they may live as long as six months.

Be a queen bee

The queen bee must save all of her energy to lay eggs, so the worker bees must do all the work in the hive. Which job would you prefer?

Toolkit
- A timer
- Friends and family
- Dice
- Crown (optional)

What to do

1 Roll a dice. Whoever throws a six gets to be queen bee first; the others have to be her workers.

2 Set the timer for five minutes. The queen can ask her workers to do anything she wants. She might ask them to: brush her hair, bring her some food, do a somersault...

3 If the queen does anything for herself — leaves her chair, plays with her hair — her turn is over. When the time's up, roll the dice and find a new queen.

Finding a new queen

When a colony becomes overcrowded, it's time for some of the bees to move out of the hive. To do so, they need a new queen bee. The bees raise a new queen bee by feeding a bee larva with extra **royal jelly**. The day before the new queen hatches, half of the worker bees fly away with the old queen, leaving the hive in search of a new home. This is called swarming.

Life in the hive

Wild honey bees often make their home in the trunk of a hollow tree. Their home is made of wax combs full of cells – some for storing honey or pollen and others for laying eggs and growing bees.

Read the story on page 36–37 to find out why bees like hollow tree trunks!

Cells full of pollen to feed the larvae.

Cells full of honey for bees to eat.

Worker bees make beeswax. They chew the wax until it becomes soft so they can shape it into hexagonal cells.

The queen bee surrounded by worker bees to help her.

Worker bees are sent out to find food.

An adult bee eats its way out of the cell (see the game of life on page 12).

Young worker bees feed the larvae.

The queen bee's cell is larger than all the others.

Try this...

Trace the below shapes six times. Cut out each shape and try putting them together to make a hive. What's wrong with the circle shape?

If we made a circle shape hive, we would need more wax to fill in the gaps!

The perfect home

Wax is very valuable to a bee. It takes eight grams of honey to make just one gram of wax. Honey combs use hexagonal cells because bees use less wax making them than if they were any other shape. It also takes less time to make, and gives them more room to store their honey.

Beekeepers

Wild honey bees live in trees but beekeepers keep some honey bees in beehives. Honey bees can make more honey than they need, so beekeepers can take any extra honey and put it in jars for people to eat.

Hive life

Beekeepers keep honey bees in hives. These special boxes feel just like living in a dark hole in a tree for a bee. The frames inside the box are lined with wax, so it is less work for the bees to build their honey combs. Bees come and go through a hole at the bottom of the hive.

Harvesting honey

When beekeepers want to take the honey from the hive, they take out the honey comb frames. While removing the frames, they wear protective suits with a veil to stop them getting stung. When they are far away from the hive, they scrape off the honey from the frames and keep it in jars.

Honey for bees

Good beekeepers are gentle with their bees and leave their bees with enough honey to get through the winter. If their bees are hungry, they will feed them.

Bees in the city

Bees do well in cities where they make lots of honey. In a city there are often all kinds of flowers available – in gardens, window boxes and pots.

When beekeepers need to remove frames from the hive they may use smoke to distract the bees.

Did you know?

Honey is really good for you. As well as being delicious to eat, it can be used to heal wounds, cuts or infections. Beeswax can be used in moisturisers, soaps, lip balm and even furniture polish!

How do bees make honey?

Honey bees make honey every spring and summer to store for winter food. A strong colony can make enough honey to survive the winter when there are fewer flowers to visit. But how do they make it?

Worker bees collect nectar from flowers and store it in their special honey stomachs. A tap at the bottom of the stomach can open and close to keep the nectar safe.

The workers then fly it back to the hive.

Worker bees spit the nectar into open cells. Other worker bees in the hive then take a drop of the nectar on their tongue. They flap their wings and make a breeze which dries off the nectar.

Look at the gooey, sticky honey!

With the work of many bees, eventually the nectar becomes gooey, sticky honey, which can be safely stored.

Done! Lots of honey in the storecupboard.

The bee then seals the cell with clean white wax, which will protect the honey as the bees' winter food store.

Are all honeys the same?

There are lots of different types of honey. Can you tell the difference?

Toolkit

- One jar of 'ordinary blended' supermarket honey
- One jar of 'special' honey (your choice)
- Two teaspoons
- Glass of water

What to do

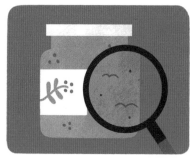

1. With your grown-up, read the label on the 'special' honey jar to find out more about it. See if you can do some research on the internet.

2. Look at the honey in the jar. What colour is it? Is it runny, jelly-like or solid?

3. Taste a teaspoon of your honey. What does it taste like? Take a sip of water and repeat with your next jar. Does it taste different?

What happens?

Nectar comes from scented flowers. The nectar flavours the honey. Every honey will taste a little different. Natural honeys can be clear or cloudy, runny or set – they are all good for you!

Lavender honey tastes of flowers.

Borage flower honey tastes light.

Chestnut tree honey tastes strong.

Manuka honey is healing but tastes horrible!

When bees were friends with elephants

A very long time ago, when the world was very young, elephants and bees were friends. Today, elephants are afraid of bees. This story from Thailand tells us why...

Long, long ago, elephants had short snouts instead of long trunks. It was hard for them to get enough food and water but they lived happily in the forest along with the bees.

One day a terrible fire swept over the land...

We can show you the way!

All the forest creatures tried to run away. The bees flew high to look for a safe place to go. They saw a river and told the elephants.

The elephants let the bees ride inside their mouths to escape the smoke. Then they walked and walked until they splashed into the river, safe at last.

When the elephants asked the bees to come out, the bees said, "No, we like it here, we want to stay." The elephants tried snorting the bees out through their snouts, but the bees would not leave.

The elephants blew so hard and for so long, that their noses stretched out into long trunks. Still the bees would not leave! So the elephants went back to the fire and breathed in the smoke. The bees didn't like that, and they finally buzzed off.

Since then bees have always built their nests in hollow trees, because it reminds them of elephants' trunks, and elephants have been afraid of bees (although their long trunks are really rather useful).

Bumble bees

Bumble bees live in colonies with a queen just like honey bees, but their families are much smaller, with only 100 to 500 bees. They usually live in old mouse holes or under long tufts of grass.

Good for us

Bumble bees are excellent pollinators of many wild plants, fruit plants and food crops. Without them, the world would look very different. What makes them such good pollinators?

We have different length tongues to reach inside different flowers.

Buff tailed bumble bee

We have hairy bodies that are very good at picking up pollen.

Red tailed bumble bee

Common carder bee

We can pollinate flowers that other bees can't. Some flowers keep their pollen tightly in the flower – we can shake it out!

Did you know?

Bees can talk to each other using smell. They leave smelly footprints on petals to let other bees know that they have taken all the nectar from a flower. The smell disappears by the time the flower is full of nectar again.

Australia does not have bumble bees, so other bees evolved to buzz pollinate plants.

Blue banded bee

Shake it like a buzzing bee

Bumble bees (and some other bees) buzz loudly when they pollinate flowers. This is called buzz pollination. Can you shake it like a buzzing bee?

Toolkit

- Tray
- Plastic beaker
- Granulated sugar
- Cling film® or sticky plastic film
- Sharp pencil
- Elastic band

What to do

1 Pour some sugar into the plastic pot. Cover the beaker with cling film and secure it with an elastic band.

2 With your adult's help, dot some tiny holes in the cling film using a sharp pencil. This is your 'pollen pot'.

3 Shake the pollen pot over a tray while making a buzzing sound.

What happens?

Tomatoes, potatoes and blueberries all need buzz pollination. These plants keep their pollen inside a pollen pot or anther. The anther has small holes in it. The pollen must be shaken out – just like your sugar. The bees take hold of the anthers and shake them really hard by vibrating their flight muscles and buzzing.

anther

stigma

seeds

nectaries

39

Make a bumble bee 'n' bee

Many bumble bees live underground. Sometimes they nest under a compost bin or shed. Why not make them a better home?

Toolkit

- Slate or tile
- 20cm wide flower pot (or bigger)
- Hosepipe – cut to about 1 metre long
- Hay or guinea pig bedding
- A spade

We like quiet places to rest where no one will disturb us!

Good places to choose are quiet, overgrown areas. You might even be able to find a quiet place at your school.

Talk to your grown-up about the best place for your Bee 'n' Bee.

What to do

1 With your grown-up, dig a hole about 5cm deep for the top of the flower pot to sit in. Turn over the flower pot and check that it fits in the hole. Then lift it out of the hole.

2 Place one end of the hose pipe in the centre of the hole. The other end will be the Bee 'n' Bee entrance.

 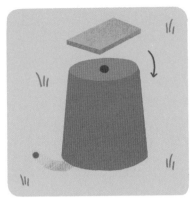 

③ Place a large handful of hay inside the flower pot, and carefully place the upturned flower pot over the hose.

④ Cover the top of the flower pot with a tile so rain will not get inside.

⑤ Cover the pipe with soil so only the entrance hole shows. Put some soil around the sides of the pot so it is secure.

What happens?
If bees move in, you may see bumble bees flying around your nest. They will land and crawl into the entrance hole. If bumble bees move into your Bee 'n' Bee please leave them be... they are happiest when left to pollinate the nearby plants.

Did you know?
The queen bumble bee lives in the nest busily laying eggs. Worker bees will help look after the nest, collecting food and looking after the new bees. Unlike the tidy honey bee, the inside of a bumble bee nest can look quite messy and disorganized!

Make a fuzzy bumble bee

Make your own lovely bumble bee with black and yellow wool.

Toolkit

- Black and yellow wool
- Cardboard
- Two googly eyes
- Tracing paper
- Scissors
- Black pipe cleaners
- PVA glue
- Stick and string

What to do

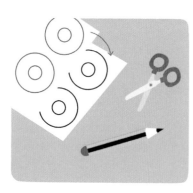

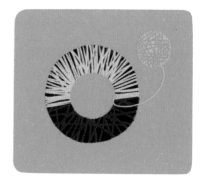

1. Trace the pompom template on page 61 and transfer it onto cardboard. Cut out your two cardboard rings.

2. Hold the two rings together. Wind the black wool around the rings and keep going until you have completely covered the cardboard. Leave the wool ends at the outside of the ring.

3. Now wind the yellow wool until you have completely covered the black wool. Leave the wool ends at the outside of the ring.

4. Then make another layer of black wool alternating with yellow wool until you fill the inner circle. Use black wool as your final layer.

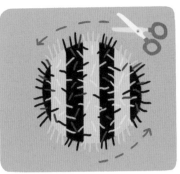

5 Ask your grown-up to help you hold the centre of the woolly ring and, using the scissors, carefully snip down the middle of the wool to reveal the two cardboard rings. Carefully loop some wool between the two rings in the centre and tie the loop tightly to fasten it.

6 Take out the rings and fluff your bee pompom. Trim off any loose ends using your scissors.

7 Trace the wing template on page 61 to make your bee wings. Cut out some legs and antennae from the pipe cleaners. Glue them on to the body, along with your googly eyes. Attach your bee to the string and tie the string to the end of the stick. Time to go on a nectar hunt!

Some bumble bees have black, brown or beige bodies. They can also have orange, yellow, cream or white stripes. Bee creative!

Make a mining bee egg burrow

Solitary bees live alone or in small groups of individual nests. Many solitary bees nest underground. See if you can make a **mining bee** egg burrow.

What to do

  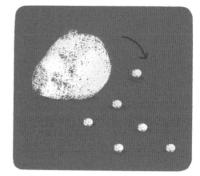

1 In a waterproof tray, mix a little water with the sand so it sticks firmly together without being too wet.

2 Using the straw, scoop out some sand to make a tube-like hole. Make a mound around the hole with the discarded sand. Repeat to make six holes.

3 Take six small amounts of cotton wool and roll them into tiny balls. These balls will be the 'eggs'.

4 Drop some glitter into each hole – this is the food the female leaves for the growing larva to eat when the egg hatches.

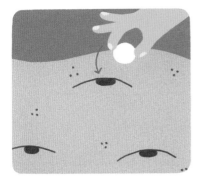  

5 Take a cotton wool egg and push it into a sand hole. Then take a handful of sand and dribble it into the hole to close it up. Repeat with two more balls.

6 Wrap a cotton wool egg in cling film. Do this for the other two eggs. Drop your wrapped eggs into the unfilled sand tubes. Dribble in some sand to fill up each hole.

7 Fill the jug with water. Now pour it over your egg-filled sand. Wait for five minutes. Then dig up your eggs.

What happens?

Some bees line their nest with liquid, which dries to give a plastic-like lining. This lining is waterproof. This means if it rains or if there is a flood the eggs are protected. The eggs you wrapped in cling film should be dry, unlike the unwrapped eggs.

Tawny mining bee

Did you know?

Inside the burrow, the female mining bee lays her egg on a ball of nectar and pollen. She does not return to care for her young bee. When the larva hatches, it will eat the food until it turns into a pupa. The pupa **hibernates** in the burrow all winter. When spring arrives, new adult mining bees emerge ready to visit fruit trees.

Build a solitary bee home

This home provides a place for solitary bees such as leafcutter and mason bees to nest in. Put it on the sunny side of a wall or fence and watch your bees move in!

Toolkit

- Scissors
- Clean 1 litre empty plastic bottle
- Paper drinking straws or hollow tubes (such as bamboo, real straw or cow parsley)
- Marker pen
- Ruler

What to do

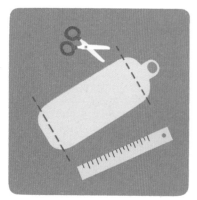

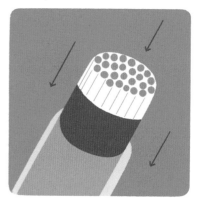

1 With your grown-up, measure 15cm from the base of your bottle. Mark a line and then cut off the top and bottom of the bottle.

2 Place a string through the centre of the bottle; leave plenty of string at each end to secure your nest to a fence.

3 Cut your drinking straws or tubes so they are 15cm in length. Pack them tightly into the bottle. If the straws aren't tightly packed they will fall out.

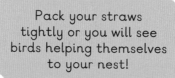

Pack your straws tightly or you will see birds helping themselves to your nest!

4 Ask your grown-up to attach your bee home securely to a sunny wall or post (at least one metre above the ground). See if you can find a sheltered spot to protect it from the wind and rain.

What happens?
You may see small bees buzzing around your nest at nesting time. If eggs have been laid by leafcutter bees, you will see leaves in the straws. If a mason bee has nested, then you will see mud in the straws. When the eggs have hatched, you will see bees fly around your nest when they emerge.

Bees don't like to build nests in a house that is too shady, wobbly or is in a windy spot.

Did you know?
Leafcutter bees separate each egg in the nest tube with pieces of leaves. Mason bees use mud walls to separate each egg. To protect the nest from predators, like birds, mason bees make a plug from mud to seal the egg tube.

Bee-ing protective

Bees only sting to protect themselves and their colony. Bees are not aggressive, unlike bad-tempered wasps, but may sting if you get too close or they feel threatened. Bee gentle!

Solitary bees don't have any honey to protect, so they have no reason to sting people.

A sting releases venom. Some people are allergic to venom and need medical help if stung.

Male bees and stingless bees cannot sting you.

Bees are busy being bees. They don't want to sting anybody.

Friendly bumble bees are more likely to wave a leg at you if you bother them than sting! They will only sting you if they need to protect their nest.

Stingless bees

Stingless bees live in tropical Australia, Africa, Asia and the Americas. Although they don't have stings, they can protect themselves by biting or chasing! They live in colonies with a queen bee and make special honey that is eaten or mixed into medical creams and drops to treat illnesses.

Honey bee queens have smooth stings so they are able to sting more than once. Queens spend almost all of their life in the hive, so a royal sting is unlikely.

It is a bad idea to play near bee hives.

If you are stung, find an adult to help you.

Honey bee workers have a barbed sting – with many small hooks along the sting. When a honey bee stings, the sting often gets stuck and left behind. A honey bee dies after losing its sting, so honey bees only use their sting to protect themselves and their colony.

Bee careful!

Beekeepers and scientists have discovered that bees are disappearing. We need bees for pollination so food can grow for us to eat. Scientists have studied bees in the wild and in beehives to find out why we have fewer bees.

There used to be lots of insects and wildlife here – now they're all gone.

Loss of habitat

Humans have destroyed many places where bees nest and flowers grow. We have built bigger towns and cities for people to live and we have turned the flower-rich countryside into one with few flowers.

Sick bees

Pests and diseases can make bees sick but we can't easily help bees once they are sick. Strong and healthy bees are less likely to get ill. To stop bees getting sick, they need a good supply of food and safe homes.

Insecticides

Insecticides kill insects, including bees. If we garden and farm without using insecticides, then we won't harm our precious bees.

Bees in the city

Imagine a city with many wildlife areas, and where buildings have window boxes and green roofs covered with plants for bees. Filled with beautiful bee-friendly plants and nesting sites, cities can be great places for bees.

SAY NO TO INSECTICIDES!

SAVE THE BEES

We can all help save bees.

- We can grow lots of flowering plants for bees.
- We can leave wild areas with long grass for bees to nest.
- We can grow areas of wild plants at the edges of farmers' fields.
- We can avoid using insecticides.
- We can make bee houses.
- We can make water dishes for bees.

Did you know?

Varroa mites have been found in most places where honey bees have been sick and died. These mites bite both baby and adult bees and they carry diseases.

Make a seed bomb

Seed bombs are great for spreading wild flowers that bees will love. Find the perfect space for your seed bomb and grow flowers for your bees.

Toolkit

- 3 tablespoons of clay powder
- 6 tablespoons of compost
- 1 packet of bee-friendly seeds
- Old mixing bowl

What to do

1 Talk to your grown-up about the perfect place for your seed bomb. It could be your garden or you could talk to your school or local council about an outdoor space to grow your bee-friendly flowers.

Be sure to use your bombs within a day of making them!

2 In a bowl, mix all the ingredients and add a little water.

Check the packet for the best time to plant your seeds.

3 Mix well using your hands. The mixture should be smooth but not sticky. Shape the mixture into small balls using your hands.

4 Place your seed bombs on the patch of soil you want the plants to grow in and water well.

What happens?

After about three weeks, the first seedlings will work their way through the seed bomb and root into the ground below. The seedlings will then grow into flowers – ready to feed your bees and provide shelter!

You can also rake your patch of soil and scatter a handful of seeds over the area. Remember to water well!

You can buy a pack of bee-friendly seeds or make up your own mixture.

Cooks and bees love herbs!

Did you know?

Bee-friendly gardeners will grow plants throughout the year to suit every kind of bee. Even if you don't have a garden or outdoor space, growing a few plants in a tub or window box will really help bees.

53

Why do bees need water?

Everyone knows that bees find their food in flowers, but bees need water too, just like other animals. Many types of bees find enough water to drink in flower nectar, but honey bees must collect water. Why?

To keep cool

In the heat of summer, the hive can get very warm, so the bees need to keep their eggs and larvae cool. Bees use their tongues to spread a thin layer of water on top of the cells. The worker bees then fan the water vigorously, so it evaporates and cools the hive.

Flower nectar is sugary water that bees love!

To soften honey

During the winter, honey can set hard and cannot be eaten. Bees use water to soften hard honey so it turns back to liquid.

Worker bee larvae are fed special 'brood food'.

To feed growing bees

One important job for a newly hatched adult bee is to nurse and feed the larvae with royal jelly and brood food. The bees have to consume lots of pollen, nectar and water to make these special foods.

Make a water dish

Honey bees need water to survive but they cannot store it. They must be able to fetch water when they need it. You can help honey bees by giving them a safe water supply.

Toolkit
- A shallow dish
- Marbles
- Water

What to do

1. Find a quiet spot where your dish will not be disturbed. A quiet flowerbed is a good place to choose.

2. Put the marbles in the dish and fill with water. Don't cover the tops of the marbles with water – the bees need somewhere safe to land.

3. Check the dish every few days to ensure there is plenty of water.

Most honey worker bees fly from the hive to gather nectar and pollen, but some worker bees collect water.

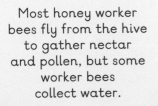

Did you know?
Bees don't like water that is too clean. They like water with stuff growing in it – like green slime! This might be because water is not usually perfectly clean in the wild so bees don't recognise the smell.

Saving bees and elephants

Bees don't just make the honey that we love to eat – they can be helpful in other ways too. Here's a story from Kenya.

Elephants walk for miles and miles to find water. They follow paths that their families have used for years. But when people needed more space to live, villages were built close to the elephant paths. People began growing food and the elephants would march into the village and eat it all up!

We can't help walking on the crops.

This was a big problem. The villagers were very cross. After a lot of thinking, somebody had an idea...

I heard that elephants are afraid of honey bees.

Let's record bees buzzing to scare the elephants away!

But it didn't work. Elephants are really very clever. They knew there weren't any real bees in the villages. They ignored the recordings and kept eating the villagers' food.

Then someone had a much better idea...

We could use real bees.

Let's put beehives on fences round our fields.

We don't want to hurt the elephants but we want to be safe too!

This time it worked. The elephants were afraid of real bees. They remembered the bees' sting and how painful that could be. They kept away.

The villagers were happy. Now they could eat their food and the honey as well! The bees made too much honey for the villagers to eat, so they started to sell it. They called it 'elephant-friendly honey', because it helped to keep the elephants and the villagers a safe distance apart.

Honey flapjacks

Impress your friends with yummy homemade honey flapjacks!

See page 34 to see how bees make honey!

What to do

You will need a grown-up to help you make this treat.

Toolkit

- 200g honey
- 200g unsalted butter
- 200g brown sugar
- 400g porridge oats
- 50g dried fruit or nuts (if you like them)
- Baking tin 20cm by 25cm
- Baking parchment

- Scissors
- Saucepan
- Wooden spoon
- Table knife
- Apron
- Oven gloves

1 Wash your hands and wear an apron to keep yourself clean.

2 Cut the baking parchment to fully line the baking tin. With your grown-up, turn on the oven to heat up to 150°C.

3 Weigh out all your ingredients and place into bowls so they are ready to use.

4 In a heavy saucepan, tip in the butter and sugar. Over a low heat stir the mixture with a wooden spoon until it is melted.

5 Turn off the heat. Add the honey and stir thoroughly. Pour in the porridge oats and dried fruit. Mix well.

6 Tip the mixture into the baking tin so it covers the base of the tin evenly. Using the back of your wooden spoon, press down gently on the top of the oat mixture.

9 When the tin and contents are cool, lift the giant flapjack out of the tin. Cut into squares. Enjoy!

7 Place the tin in the oven for 40 minutes. (Now is a good time to help your grown-up with the washing up!)

8 With your grown-up, and wearing oven gloves, lift out the tin and leave it to cool.

Templates

Page 16.

Page 18.

Page 21.

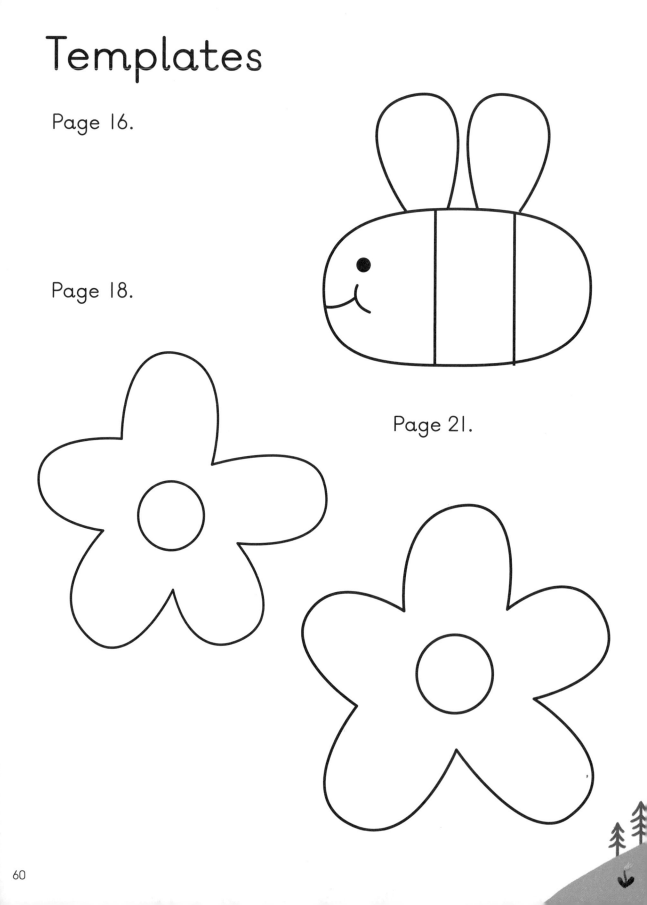

Page 42.

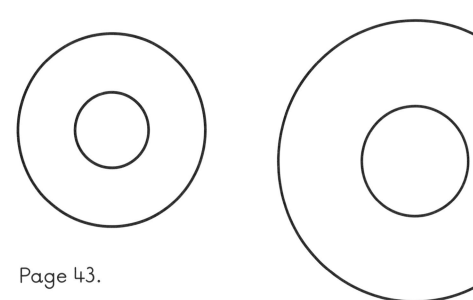

Page 43.

Glossary

Anther Part of a plant where pollen is made.

Brood food Special food made by worker honey bees that is fed to bee larvae (baby bees).

Bumble bees Big, fat, hairy bees that buzz pollinate plants. In summer they live in families with a queen bee. In winter, the queen bumble bee lives alone.

Carbohydrates Different types of sugar and starch used by animals for energy. Bees only eat sugars found in nectar and honey.

Colony A family of bees, with a queen and female worker bees.

Drones Male bees. They have no sting.

Egg Laid by a female bee, this is the start of a bee's life. In honey bees, bumble bees and stingless bees, eggs are laid by queen bees.

Fertilization The moment when a new seed or egg begins life.

Hibernation A time in winter when the bees go to sleep. Honey bees do not hibernate but huddle together to keep warm in the colony.

Honey Sweet and sticky food made by bees from flower nectar. It is good to eat if you are a bee or a human.

Honey bees Bees that live in a colony or family and who make enough honey to feed their family through the winter, when there aren't many flowers to visit.

Insecticides Chemicals used by gardeners and growers to kill insects – often to make plants grow better food for us to eat. Sadly, some insecticides kill bees.

Larva A baby bee that has hatched from an egg and looks like a small worm.

Mandibles The jaws of a bee used to chew up food and to make things.

Mining bees Solitary bees that dig or mine holes to make a nest.

Nectar A sweet and watery food made by flowers. It is eaten by bees and is used by some bees to make honey.

Nectary / nectaries The part of the plant, usually in the flower, that makes nectar.

Pollen Protein-rich food for bees made in the anthers of flowers. Pollen is needed by plants to make seeds.

Pollination The carrying of pollen from the anthers to the stigma on another plant. After a plant is pollinated, its seeds will be fertilized and begin life.

Proboscis A bee's tongue which is used just like a straw. It is used to suck up and drink nectar or honey.

Queen bee The special female bee that lays eggs in honey bee, bumble bee and stingless bee colonies.

Royal jelly A special bee food made by worker honey bees. A little royal jelly is fed to all baby bees but most is fed to baby queen bees. Adult queen bees eat it too.

Seeds Made when a flower is fertilized. A new plant will grow from a seed. Some seeds are held inside a fruit or nut.

Solitary bees Many solitary bees are very small and live or nest alone. Leafcutter, mason and mining bees are all types of solitary bee.

Stigma The part of the plant where pollen must go for pollination to happen.

Stingless bees Bees that cannot sting but can bite to protect themselves. They live in tropical places where they live in colonies and make honey.

Ultra-violet (UV) light A special light that we can't see but that can damage our eyes, so we need to wear sunglasses on sunny days. Bees can see ultra-violet light as bee purple.

Wax Made by bees and used to build brood combs for raising baby bees and honey comb for storing honey. We use wax to make candles.

Worker bees Female bees in honey bee, bumble bee and stingless bee families who do all the work!

Bee names

Latin name	Common name
Amegilla cingulata	Blue banded bee
Andrena fulva	Tawny mining bee
Anthophora plumipes	Hairy footed flower bee
Apis dorsata	Giant honey bee
Apis florea	Red dwarf honey bee
Apis mellifera	Western honey bee
Bombus lapidarius	Red tailed bumble bee
Bombus pascuorum	Common carder bee
Bombus pensylvanicus	American bumble bee
Bombus terrestris	Buff tailed bumble bee
Habropoda laboriosa	South Eastern blueberry bee
Megachile centuncularis	Leafcutter bee
Megachile pluto	Wallace's giant bee
Melipona beecheii	Xunan kab or royal lady bee
Tetragonisca angustula	Jataí bee
Tetragonula carbonaria	Sugar bag bee

Index

Quarto is the authority on a wide range of topics.
Quarto educates, entertains and enriches the lives of our readers—enthusiasts and lovers of hands-on living. www.quartoknows.com

Author: Andrea Quigley
Illustrator: Pau Morgan
Consultant: Norman Carreck
Editors: Sophie Hallam & Carly Madden
Designer: Clare Barber

Copyright © QED Publishing 2017

First published in the UK in 2017 by
QED Publishing
Part of The Quarto Group
The Old Brewery
6 Blundell Street
London, N7 9BH

A catalogue record for this book is available from the British Library.

ISBN 978 1 78493 789 8

Printed in China